CORNELL DYER AND THE NEVER ROBBERS

An *Adventures of Cornell Dyer* supernatural mystery

Denise M. Baran-Unland

In collaboration with Timothy M. Baran

Illustrated by Sue Midlock

CORNELL DYER AND THE NEVER ROBBERS
Copyright © 2019 by Denise M. Baran-Unland
All rights reserved. No part of this book may be reproduced, scanned, or distributed in any printed or electronic form without permission.
Printed in the United States of America
ISBN: 978-1-949777-08-6

This book is lovingly dedicated to the reader, whoever you might be.

We all have our time machines, don't we. Those that take us back are memories...And those that carry us forward, are dreams. - H.G. Wells

TABLE OF CONTENTS

Prologue

Chapter 1: Dyer Straits

Chapter 2: The Bank That Wasn't

Chapter 3: The Never Robbers

Chapter 4: A Curious Case of Molly Burton

Chapter 5: On the Other Side of Time

Chapter 6: It's More Than a Tire Swing

Chapter 7: That Ole Dirt Road

Chapter 8: A Trip to 1879

Chapter 9: Before the Thunder

Chapter 10: She Was Always Like That

Epilogue

PROLOGUE

The West Virginian estate was a paradigm of blissful perfection.

The manicured grounds extended for miles and showcased fragrant gardens, well-trodden walking paths, and trickling, sparkling, blue-green streams.

A large white mansion ruled those grounds. Inside that mansion, servants supplied every comfort imaginable.

Hot meals on cold days. Cool drinks on warm days.

Baths the right temperature.

Hand-sewn clean, starched, stylish clothing.

Billowy pillows and downy quilts.
Not a smidgen of dust anywhere.
The boy's hideaway lay to the rear of the estate, near Dyer Lane and in a well-constructed white gazebo.
The boy often retreated to this gazebo with a book, his favorite spot for reading in the vast wonderland.
He lounged there now, happily lost in tales of pirates and hidden treasures, unhampered by the approaching dusk and reveling in the cool breeze.
Next to the gazebo stood a tall pole.
Topping the pole was a globe.
The globe glowed with a soft light, enough to illuminate the words on the page.
In the distance, he heard his nanny ringing the dinner bell and calling his name. He ignored the call, as he ignored the call every evening.
The boy turned a page.
A boom sounded in the distance.
The boy glanced up. An approaching storm? A cannon?
No wind.
No more bell.
No calling of his name or trickling of

the stream.

His neck prickled.

The bulb shone with brilliant light.

When the nanny arrived with her lantern, she only saw shattered glass on the path, soot inside the gazebo, and the abandoned copy of *Treasure Island*.

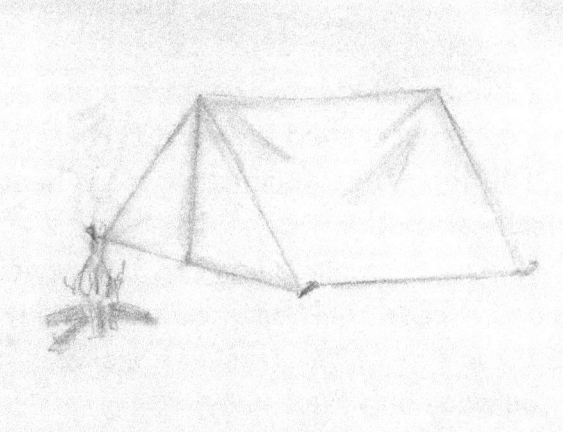

CHAPTER ONE: DYER STRAIGHTS

Cornell Dyer felt very miserable indeed.

For over two hours, he'd trudged down the dusty shoulder of Highway 52, blazer slung over his shoulder, in pursuit of his motor home and the thieves who drove away with it.

He spun around in time to see his motor home speeding away.
In the back, a girl with curly red hair held up a sign.
The sign read: HELP ME!

The blinding sun stung Cornell's eyes, even as sweat rolled into them from his forehead, and scorched his bare forearms.

The top of his damp curly black head practically sizzled in the heat.

His stomach rumbled. The jelly snack cakes and cheese curls he'd rummaged out of the glove box of the thieves' broken-down car were only a memory.

His dry mouth tasted like a wad of cotton. The bottle of cream soda he'd retrieved from under the car's front seat was also a memory.

How dare anyone, much less a group of anyones, steal the motor home belonging to the great Professor Cornell Dyer, supernatural super sleuth of supernatural mysteries?

Just wait until he caught up with them. Just wait.

His motor home had better be intact. Not not one scratch. Not one dent. Not one fizzy potion or sandwich cookie missing.

He'd long passed the Indiana border. But the farther he walked, the stranger the landscape became.

No cars zoomed past.

No people on bicycles whizzed past.

No joggers zipped past.

The air was strangely silent. No hum of an airplane or twitter of birds.

Cornell reached inside his pocket for his enchanted everywhere map and brought up gloop.

The gloop smelled bad and smeared the lines of the map into all the wrong directions.

Cornell had forgotten, again, to throw away the old mayonnaise packets. Well, when one is busying solving important supernatural mysteries, one cannot remember everything.

He shoved the map back inside his pocket and felt it squoosh against the mayonnaise. But Cornell did not believe in littering.

Then he squatted, dragged his fingers across a grassy patch to remove the smelly goop, and resumed his trudge.

He hoped the girl was unharmed, but she, at least, was inside his motor home. Cornell trusted the motor home to protect her.

As soon as Cornell reached a town, he

would go straight to the police. He would report the theft, and he would report the kidnapping.

If he had known thieves would steal his motor home, he would not have left Larry the Llama in Marbleheart.

If he still had Larry, he would not be hot, tired, and still walking.

But, no, the llama wanted to stay with Mrs. Horsehair. Ungrateful beast.

The view up ahead blurred into squiggles.

Cornell stopped.

He shaded his eyes.

He squinted through the sunlight.

And then he blinked. Was that a lake?

Yes, that was definitely a lake, shimmering irresistibly, just past the highway.

Cornell swallowed a very dry swallow.

It's a mirage, Cornell told himself. It's an optical illusion on the road because the air is too hot, and the sky is too bright.

But then he saw the trees, an entire wooded expanse. He heard the splashing of waves, the tweeting of birds, the croaking of frogs.

He dove through the brush toward the lake. Faster and faster he tromped through the weeds, as fast as he tired legs would take him. The sounds grew fainter; the sun burned hotter.

Cornell found only the highway, with not even a mud puddle to reward his efforts.

Frustrated, irritated, hungry, and parched, Cornell turned back, and there it was: a metal lawn chair with green vinyl slats, unfolded and ready for use, right in the middle of the woods.

Beyond the chair lay the lake.

Someone had dug a hole next to the chair. Beside the chair, someone had piled wood, tinder, and a small box of matches.

Next to the hole sat a foam cooler. Cornell opened it and found a covered dinner plate, topped with a folded index card.

Cornell opened the card and read in beautiful Spencerian script:

I don't like to be hungry or uncomfortable either. M.O.

Then Cornell lifted the lid to the dinner plate. He found a giant steak, well done and still hot; an enormous mound of fluffy white mashed potatoes dripping with yellow butter and brown gravy, also still hot; and glazed string beans topped with almonds.

Yes, the beans were hot, just as if they'd come right off the stove.

So were the dinner rolls, six in all.

Four bottles of icy cold orange drink kept the dinner plate company, along with a brand-new bottle opener.

Cornell eased into the chair, opened a bottle, and slurped and slurped. Sighing happily, he set the drink on the grass, unrolled the napkin, and dove into the dinner.

For many hours after the food was gone, Cornell lounged in the chair, basking in the lake, the sun that eventually began to set, and the light breeze cooling his sunburnt skin.

As he basked, Cornell thought about his stolen motor home, and the gears cranked in his head.

When the sun and the temperatures dipped, Cornell lit the fire. He thought about the kidnapped girl, and the best way to rescue her.

The crackling of the fire, and the

sloshing of the waves relaxed Cornell's mind and body.

Tomorrow, he thought sleepily. Tomorrow I will solve all supernatural mysteries.

When he awakened, night had settled over the lake and land. The fire had burned to embers.

A folded note rested on his lap. Scratching his matted curls, Cornell opened the note, and held it close to his eyes to read the Spencerian script in the dark.

You shouldn't have to sleep under the stars. M.O.

That's when Cornell saw, far from the fire, a pitched tent with its front flaps opened in a welcoming way.

After a big stretch and a bigger yawn, Cornell fell off the chair, crawled to the shelter, and passed out on top of the blankets.

"Cornell!"
He opened his eyes. A large grizzly

bear loomed over him.

"Cornell!"

A talking grizzly bear?

This was almost as strange as the singing salamander he encountered at Falls Lake, the one practicing to be an opera star.

"Let's go," the grizzly said.

Cornell peered closer. This wasn't a grizzly but a man, a great burly man standing on the same grass where Cornell was lying.

For the blankets and tent was gone, and the chair, fire pit, and foam cooler was also gone.

The lake was still there, calm and rippling in the morning sun.

The motor home was still gone, too, but at least Cornell was working on getting that back.

Cornell leaped to his feet.

"Who are you?" Cornell demanded.

"I run a taxi service."

The man held out a crumpled piece of paper with scrawling, sloppy penmanship.

"The guy who summoned me said he didn't want to leave you lying in the dirt. And he's sorry about taking your motor home."

CHAPTER TWO: THE BANK THAT WASN'T

Chewing on a cigar the entire way, the taxi driver roared into town and then screeched to a stop.

Cornell reached for his wallet and then realized his wallet was in the motor home.

"Sir, about the bill..." Cornell began.

"No charge!" the driver exclaimed.

"Hmmm," Cornell said as he opened the car door and stepped onto the sidewalk.

He turned to thank the driver.

But the driver removed his cigar, spat on the sidewalk, and gave a friendly wave as he sped away in a choking cloud of exhaust.

When the haze cleared, and after Cornell stopped coughing, Cornell read the road sign: Welcome to Prospect, Indiana. Established December 12,1816.

Then he studied his surroundings for clues.

The buildings had blue awnings and fresh white paint. The streets gleamed with clean black tar.

To his right, a firefighter was lifting a mewing kitten out of a leafy tree.

To his left, a police officer with a shiny silver whistle stood on the corner. With a smile, the officer guided cars and pedestrians to their destinations.

Beyond the shops, Cornell heard the buzz of lawnmowers and the happy shouts of children engaged in a games of jump rope and baseball.

Friendly people passed him on all sides, beaming as they waved or tipped their hats to him.

Cornell felt as relaxed as he had last night by the lake. But as he strolled, he kept a sharp watch for his motor home.

A loud jangling rent the air. The

policeman blew on his whistle with piercing blows. Squad cars with blaring sirens sped toward a bright white building: The First Bank of Prospect.

Policeman with silver badges on their chests and silver cuffs hanging from their belts poured out of the cars and toward the bank.

Beyond the bank, parked in a shady grove of trees, was the motor home!

As Cornell pushed his way through the thickening crowds, four robbers wearing black masks strolled out of the bank carrying big white sacks, each with a large green dollar sign printed on the front.

One man, short and pudgy, whipped off his mask, exposing his smirk and balding black hair.

"Aw, they've caught us," the short and pudgy man said. "You might as well take your masks off."

"Put your hands up!" one officer cried.

"Who do you think you are, bringing trouble to Prospect, Indiana?" a second officer shouted.

"I'm Bishop Caffety," the short man said with a wide grin, pointing to his

17

companions. "And this Molly Burton, Mike Olsen, and Danny Tyler. We're the Never Robbers. And we haven't been hitting up banks all over the state."

Cornell gasped.

Mike Olsen, with his brown hair and freckles, was not too short and not too tall. He wasn't fat, and he wasn't thin. He was the type of person who could get lost in a crowd unless someone was specifically looking for him, which no one was.

Danny Tyler was very tall, very thin. He had a beard, a black suit, a stovetop hat, and he looked like Abraham Lincoln.

Cornell recognized Molly Burton, which is why he gasped. This young woman with curly reddish-blonde hair, blue eyes, and porcelain skin, was the same girl who'd held up the *HELP ME!* sign in the rear window of the motor home as it had sped away.

"I'll make a deal with you," Bishop Cafferty said as he eyed the officers. "We'll put the money down if you let us drive away in our motor home."

"Your motor home!" Cornell shrieked as he lunged forward. "How dare you! That's

MY motor home!"

Bishop Cafferty nimbly hopped to one side, and Cornell crashed to the ground. A flashlight bounced out of Cornell's pocket and clicked on. Thunder rumbled in the background.

While murmurs of "Is a storm coming?" spread through the crowd, Bishop Cafferty tossed up the money. The flashlight blazed with blinding white light.

The light died.

Cornell was lying on the ground with a scraped elbow and a dead flashlight.

HONK! HONK-HONK!

Cornell scrambled to his feet. The taxi driver was chewing on his cigar and glaring at Cornell. The bank was gone.

"Where's the bank?" Cornell pointed to the bank-sized singed spot where, just a few moments ago, the white building proudly stood.

The taxi driver snorted. "Do your banking in the next town!"

He spat on the sidewalk and sped away in a black suffocating cloud.

Cornell hurried to the police officer, who irritably blew on his whistle.

"Where is the bank?" Cornell demanded.

"What bank?" the officer snarled.

"THAT bank! And the four bank robbers!"

"Bank robbers! We're too far north for bank robbers! We leave that for central Indiana!"

The officer guffawed at his lame joke.

"Sir, I am the great Professor Cornell Dyer. I am a supernatural super sleuth who solves supernatural mysteries. I can clearly see the spot where a bank once stood. Don't deny it!"

The officer blew hard on his whistle, and a car skidded to a stop.

"I'm not denying anything! The bookkeeper, working by candlelight one night when the electric went out, accidentally tipped over the candle and burned the bank down! We have no bank!"

A man ran up to Cornell. "Sir, are you the world famous Professor Cornell Dyer?"

"I am."

He thrust out an envelope. "You have a letter."

Cornell ripped open the letter, pulled out a little white card, and read in Spencerian script:

You shouldn't litter in front of a police officer. M.O.

Cornell glanced down. He had accidentally dropped the envelope.
As Cornell bent to retrieve it, the officer snapped a set of cuffs around Cornell's wrists.
"We don't tolerate littering in Prospect," the officer said. "I'm taking you to jail."

CHAPTER THREE: THE NEVER ROBBERS

For the second time in as many days, Cornell woke up with a start.

Scattered across the lumpy bed in the dark cell was the remains of that night's fried chicken dinner, courtesy of the jailor's wife.

"Hiya, chump!"

Cornell looked up at the window and saw the taunting grin of Bishop Cafferty, who had his nose pressed against the glass.

"Rotting away in jail, are we?"

"I'm not answering your questions until I get my motor home back, and you pay for your crimes."

"Can't get caught by the police when I've never done anything wrong, nyah, nyah."

But Cornell had more pressing concerns than heckling from a thief. Cornell's wristwatch said midnight, and the moon in the black sky proved it.

The watch in his shoe said midnight. The watch inside his belt buckle said midnight. The watch inside his lapel said midnight.

But his gold pocket watch said 6:15.

Cornell scowled. Impossible! All of his clocks and watches always kept perfect time. Especially his old gold pocket watch.

"You remember me right, Professor?"

But Cornell coolly replied, "How many crates are you standing on, little man?"

Bishop Cafferty's smile fled. "Ha, ha, you're hilarious!" He wagged a fat finger. "Look at you, the great Professor Cornell Dyer, locked up for breaking the law. You're not as smart as you look."

A second voice outside whispered, "Should we tell him they don't lock the cells at night?"

Bishop Cafferty slapped his forehead. "Mike!"

Cornell leaped to the door and slid the rails aside. Then he sprinted out of the jail and straight to the grove of trees where his motor home was still parked.

Blocking the entryway were all four Never Robbers.

"Move!" Cornell cried.

"No," Bishop Cafferty said.

"Do you know who I am?" Cornell exclaimed.

"You're the great Cornell Dyer," Bishop Cafferty sneered.

"That's 'Professor' Cornell Dyer," Cornell said.

"You're a super sleuth," Danny Tyler said.

"You solve supernatural mysteries," Mike Olsen said.

Molly didn't answer. She was gone.

"Move!"

Cornell patted his pockets for his "get out of my way" card, squishing mayonnaise packets with every pat.

"If you don't move, I'll..."

Bishop Cafferty flapped his hands. "Easy, easy, Professor. You're making us out to be worse than we really are."

"You've stolen my motor home, robbed a bank, and a girl who begged for my help is missing once again! Now for the last time..."

Bishop Cafferty sighed. He also looked amused.

"Professor," Bishop Cafferty said. "We only take what we need plus a little extra. The girl is one of us. She doesn't need your help or anyone's help."

"Aha!"

Cornell pulled the card, and a mayonnaise packet, out of his back pocket.

"I, the great Professor Cornell Dyer, command..."

Bishop Cafferty's smirk fled, and he held up his hands to ward off the spell.

"Hold on, Professor, we just want to talk to you," Bishop Cafferty said.

"...you to mo..."

"We want to know how you can remember the motor home ever existed and how you can know us from a bank robbery that never took place."

Cornell lowered the card. "What?"

"We want to know how you can remember what never existed."

Danny Tyler and Mike Olsen nodded to

show they agreed with Bishop Cafferty.

Cornell took a deep breath. He was hungry, thirsty, tired, and really, really, really irritated with the Never Robbers.

"My motor home is right here. Clearly, you stole it."

Bishop Cafferty spread out his palms. "You're an interesting bird, Professor, and since you're one of the few people who know about us, we want to chat with you. Please." He gestured to the door. "Do come into my motor home."

Cornell spluttered, "You're motor home? *You're motor home?*"

Bishop Cafferty pulled out Cornell's missing keys and jangled them before Cornell's face.

"If it's your motor home, why not open the door?"

Danny Tyler and Mike Olsen slapped their foreheads.

"Every time!" Danny Tyler exclaimed.

"Every time!" Mike Olsen echoed. "Every time we come here, the Professor and Bishop Cafferty argue about the motor home."

Cornell stooped down, reached under

the step, and pulled out a little magnetic box. He opened the box and removed the spare key.

Bishop Cafferty's jaw dropped.

"Don't look so surprised," Danny Tyler said. "He does it every time."

"What do you mean, 'every time?'" Cornell asked as he unlocked the door.

The minute he stepped inside, Cornell gasped. And it was not a happy gasp.

"Oh, no!" he cried. "What did you do?"

Molly Brown was arranging a vase of wild daisies in the center of the kitchen table.

"I cleaned the motor home and put all the junk away," Molly said with a sweet smile. "To make it more livable."

"You did WHAT???"

Every book was now neatly lined up on every shelf, which smelled of lemon furniture polish. He saw the lines of the carpet sweeper on his carpet where he used to stack boxes and where his collection of pixies used to roam.

Even worse, Cornell did not see a single doughnut box or potato chip can on the counter. But he did see a bowl of apples, oranges, and bananas.

Pictures of prairies and old barns hung on the walls instead of the newspaper clippings detailing his exploits.

"I had almost an entire wall papered!" Cornell exploded.

"That's not important now," Bishop Cafferty said. "We've reset this day ten times already just so we could talk, and we've only got a narrow bit of time left."

"Reset the day?"

"Yes, Professor," Molly said. "This isn't the first time we've done this. Let's sit at the table and have lunch."

Molly opened the oven door and brought out a platter of grilled cheese sandwiches and placed them on the table.

She did the same with a pot of tomato soup. Then she went to the refrigerator. Five frosted glasses of water stood on the racks. Each glass had a lemon wedge on the rim.

Molly set the glasses at each table place. Then she joined the others.

After a few bites of his sandwich, Bishop Cafferty said with his mouth full, "Listen, Professor. We're just ordinary, but slightly unique, people. We don't know how we got here, but we've doing the things we do for a very long time. We want you, the great Professor Cornell Dyer, to solve the mystery."

Cornell stuffed the crust in his mouth and reached for another sandwich. "Go on."

Bishop Cafferty glanced at the other Never Robbers, who nodded back at him.

"I used to be a dentist," Bishop Cafferty said. "Mike Olsen grew up in some ritzy place awhile back, but he doesn't remember too much of it. Danny Tyler won't tell us much about him. He said if we don't recognize him, we're all uneducated."

Bishop Cafferty jerked his head toward the girl. "And then we have Molly Brown."

Cornell reached for the ladle, glancing at Molly, who was eating with gusto and looking as if she was having a good time.

He was not happy with Molly.

"Why did you beg for my help?" Cornell asked Molly. "You don't look as if you need help."

Bishop Cafferty's face flushed. "Because sometimes this loudmouthed little girl..."

"You're being stubborn, Bishop," Danny Tyler said in a deep, low voice. "She did the right thing."

Cornell ran his hand through his still-dusty, still-matted black curls. "I'm so confused. Stop talking nonsense and give me facts."

He removed his notebook and ballpoint pen from his T-shirt pocket. Cornell opened the notebook to a fresh page and clicked the pen on.

Mike Olsen piped up. "Professor, Molly does need help. We all need help. And every time we go looking for it, we keep bumping into you. And the motor home is always in the same spot."

"Sir, we've never met!"

"Wrong!" Danny Tyler said.

Mike pointed to Danny Tyler and then to Bishop Cafferty.

"You see, Professor, the three of us have been together for a very, very long time. Molly is the new addition. We just met her today. But today was years ago...I think."

Danny Tyler leaned forward. "We do our best to keep track of it. But jumping around makes it a little hard sometimes."

"Eureka! You're talking about time travel!"

Mike Olsen shook his head. "We're not talking about time travel. We're talking about something that isn't anymore, something different people remember differently. But we've hit a little snag."

"What snag?" Cornell asked, pen poised.

"We've all experienced something that is, but not anymore, with people remembering it in various ways. But we're stuck with the original memories, all of the original memories in all their different forms."

Cornell, even more confused, wrote that down.

Mike Olsen took a sip of water. "We wake up, and the day has changed. But we've also learned how to make it change, depending on the cards we're dealt, and if we like them or not. Sometimes we play them, and sometimes we don't."

Danny Tyler nodded his head and stroked his beard.

"It's been kind of fun remembering

things that aren't fun anymore and changing them around." Mike Olsen's face darkened. "But we're getting older."

"We're all getting older," Cornell scoffed.

"Just this morning," Mike Olsen said, ignoring Cornell's comment, "Bishop Cafferty had a full head of hair. Danny didn't have a lick of gray hair, and I was almost a teenager."

Cornell wrote that down.

"The only one who hasn't changed is Molly, but she's new to our group," Mike Olsen continued. "So maybe what's happening to us isn't happening to her yet."

Cornell wrote that down. "Sure sounds like time travel to me."

"It's not time travel," Danny said sternly. "No one should mess with time travel. We know who you are. But we needed to meet you before you start exploring mountains."

Cornell laughed hard. "Mountains! In Indiana?"

Mike Olsen winked at Danny Tyler. "Professor, that's another story for another time. Today, it's about why we want to talk to you. Many times we've met you and talked to you, but the next day you don't remember us. So we decided to change the equation a bit."

Cornell wrote that down.

"Professor," Danny Tyler said. "Do you have a match?"

Molly jumped up. "I'll get it! I found a box with lots of old matches when I was cleaning."

Cornell scowled. He did not write that down.

Molly returned with a book of matches and handed it to Danny Tyler.

Danny Tyler opened the book and tore out a match. He closed the book and struck the match. A tiny flame appeared.

"Watch," Danny Tyler said, stretching out his arm.

Cornell watched. The tiny flicker grew larger and brighter, brighter and larger.

Far in the distance came a rumbling sound, the same sound Cornell heard at the bank.

The match popped.

"Let's go outside," Danny Tyler said as he rose from his chair.

Danny Tyler led the way, Cornell and the others filed out after him.

As they moved away from motor home, Cornell held his sleeve over his nose. "What is that terrible smell?"

"Garbage," Danny Tyler said, shuffling and rubbing his lower back.

"This is Prospect, Indian, the way we remember it," Mike Olsen said. "We've never brought you here. And now we're paying the price."

Mike Olsen, too, walked slower, and he had a paunch around his middle.

Bishop Cafferty's bald spot over took the top of his head. The bald spot was speckled with brown spots. He only had hair above his ears, and that hair was gray.

Molly's reddish-blonde curls drooped.

"What's happening?" Cornell asked.

"Keep walking," Danny Tyler said.

That was easy because everyone except Cornell and Molly ambled very, very slowly.

After a long while, the small party finally arrived at the town square.

Cornell gasped again, annoyed that gasping was becoming a habit for him.

The houses and the neighborhoods were gone. The shops were boarded up. The streets were littered with garbage.

"What did you do?" Cornell cried. "What did you do to these people and their clean, happy town?"

"We made it better," Danny Tyler said.

"This is not better!"

Cornell stomped his foot so they could see he was angry with them.

Mike Olsen's shoulders slumped. His face had a few wrinkles. "Sure it is, Professor. Prospect, Indiana got hit hard during the Great Depression. It's only bank closed, and that hurt a lot of people."

Bishop Cafferty said, "It's like this, Professor. We've been jumping to a hundred different versions of Prospect, Indiana. Except none of these versions ever existed. Until we bring them back. We do it for them."

"You robbed the bank," Cornell said.

Danny Tyler shook his head. "Can't rob what isn't there."

Bishop Cafferty sneered, "Do you remember it being built?"

35

Mike Olsen quickly added, "But we're putting it there to make sure people have it."

Cornell started for his notebook and pen and then changed his mind.

"I'm so confused," Cornell said.

Danny Tyler placed a gnarled hand on Cornell's shoulder. "Imagination and memories are a potent combination. In my day people said I was wise. So I've formulated this theory. I think Bishop, Mike, and I are in this situation together because we share a similar memory. And I think we're aging fast today because we're disappearing from memory."

"Eureka!" Cornell cried. "Come with me!"

He ran back to the motor home and straight for his bedroom closet. He pulled out a box, dumped it on the floor, and pawed through its contents.

Nope!

Cornell grabbed another box and repeated his actions.

Nope again!

Finally, Cornell reached the last box and found it.

By now the group had returned. All of them, except Molly, looked very old.

Cornell waved the yellowed, smudged, taped pamphlet.

"Here it is!" Cornell cried. "It's the Madeline effect!"

Bishop Cafferty loudly sighed. "What's the Madeline effect?"

Cornell held up the pamphlet. "The Madeline effect was named after a little girl who simply vanished one day. Except 62 percent of people remember seeing her the day before her disappearance, and the others swore they never saw her again.

"A few years later she bought a house that wasn't there. At least that's how 48 percent of people remember it. No one knows what happened. Some say she's still out there somewhere, and others don't remember her because she's wiped from their memory. But that doesn't mean she's not somewhere.

"But even for the people who remember Madeline, she lives only on the tip of their memory, jut out of reach. These people have collectively lost their memories. A memory that, as group, they cannot remember.

"But they almost remember it nearly the same way, which is why they can change it to the way people remember it. All of you..."

Cornell pointed at Bishop Cafferty, then to Danny Tyler, and then to Mike Olsen. "All of you must share a memory that's nearly the same."

Bishop Cafferty twisted his mouth in deep thought.

"Well," Bishop Cafferty said slowly. "I'm a dentist. I was at my office peering into patient's mouth when I heard a little thunder, and the light above the patient grew really bright.

"Then the light bulb popped; I smelled the singed rubber on my shoes, and I was sitting in a restaurant booth with Danny Tyler and Mike Olsen."

Cornell quickly wrote that down. "What about Danny Tyler?"

"I was sitting in a theater with my wife," Danny Tyler said. "I heard thunder in the back of my head, and the lights above the stage grew really bright. As they exploded, I found myself sitting in the same restaurant with Bishop and Mike."

Cornell nodded as he wrote that down. "And Mike Olsen?"

"I was called into the house for dinner," Mike Olsen said. "I didn't want to go because I was reading a good book. Then I heard thunder, and the outdoor light grew very extremely bright. As it popped, I was sitting in the booth next to Bishop and Danny."

Cornell was nodding very hard as he wrote that down.

"Here's the strange part, Professor," Mike Olsen continued. "It felt as if we'd always been together. Not long after that, we started changing people's minds and memories. And we've been doing that for a really, really long time."

Cornell stopped writing. "And you've survived by robbing banks."

"Wrong!" Bishop Cafferty exclaimed. "We've survived by robbing no banks. If the banks never existed, or if people don't remember the banks, or their money, it's not really a bank robbery."

"Besides," Mike chimed in. "We've done a lot of good with that money."

"He's right," Danny Tyler added. "We've built schools, hospitals, churches, orphanages, and humane societies."

"And banks!" Bishop Cafferty cried. "Don't forget banks!"

Danny Tyler ignored him. "We've helped the poor with food, clothing, shelter, and education."

"And we've jumped all over time to do it," Mike Olsen said. "But most importantly, Professor, we've helped people forget their hardships, so that all they remember..."

"That's it!" Cornell cried excitedly. "Everyone perceives time as a line. But time is really an open space. So every now and then, a memory can span across time and affect wide amounts of people."

"...which isn't time travel," Danny Tyler insisted.

Cornell stretched his arms out very wide. "What's happening is the whole world experiencing the Madeline effect, and we are outside of it. And Molly here..."

He turned and pointed at Molly.

But Molly was gone.

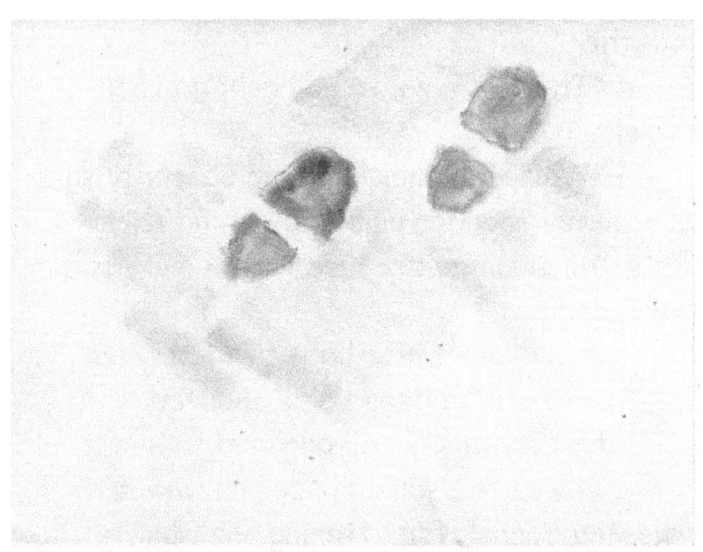

CHAPTER FOUR: A CURIOUS CASE OF MOLY BURTON

Cornell looked past his crooked, wrinkled finger to the wisp of smoking rising from the place Molly had recently stood.

He looked at the other three Never Robbers and gasped.

Yes, Cornell gasped again.

All three looked very old and very frail.

"What happened?" Danny Tyler asked, blinking in disbelief. "Did Molly fade from memory?"

Mike Olsen looked scared. "We've never traveled separately since we've been together."

"Then we have to go back!" Cornell exclaimed.

"Wait, schumck," Bishop Cafferty said as faraway thunder rumbled behind them. "It's still smoking because the memory is fresh and hot."

A brilliant white light blinded them.

"Freeze!" a deep voice shouted.

Not again, Cornell groaned to himself.

It was the same policeman who arrested Cornell for littering. He was chewing on a chicken leg and searching them with his flashlight, not the cheap snow gun the Never Robbers had used on him when they had stolen the motor home.

"What's wrong?" Cornell asked.

"Been a jail break," the policeman said. "Who are you? Why are you here in the middle of the night?"

By the time the flashlight popped, daylight had returned to Prospect, Indiana.

The buildings had blue awnings and fresh white paint. The streets gleamed with clean black tar.

To his right, a firefighter was lifting a mewing kitten out of a leafy tree.

To his left, a police officer with a shiny silver whistle stood on the corner. With a smile, the officer guided cars and pedestrians to their destinations

Beyond the shops, Cornell heard the hum of lawnmowers and the happy shouts of children engaged in a games of jump rope and baseball.

Friendly people passed him on all sides, beaming as they waved or tipped their hats to him.

In fact, everything and everyone looked exactly the way Cornell first saw it.

Except for two things.

One, a bright red ribbon hung across the front doors of the bright, white building called The First Bank of Prospect.

Two, each person, as they walked, left behind soot, which slowly vanished as they walked.

Cornell gasped. "I can see their memories!"

He looked down at his feet and the feet of the other three Never Robbers, white-haired, wrinkled, and bent with painful arthritis. "I'm outside the Madeline effect!"

"Because no one remembers us,"

Danny Tyler said.

Cornell looked at the officer, and their eyes met. Immediately the officer strode over to Cornell.

Here we go again, Cornell thought.

Aloud, Cornell said in a weak voice, so weak it took plenty of effort to speak, "Sir, are you missing something?"

The officer looked puzzled. "You look like someone who litters." He peered closer. "Maybe not, though." Then he shook his head. "No, I don't know you at all."

He turned away and hurried back to his post.

"Professor," Danny Tyler said in an old, hoarse voice. "We really need to find Molly Burton. I think we're aging fast because she's not here."

Cornell held up a hand, the one not holding the notebook and ballpoint pen. "Hey, this is your show. You stole my motor home. I now have it back. Molly Burton pleaded for help. But she didn't need help. I was tricked. My work here is fini..."

His voice trailed off as he saw his hands: gnarled and shaking. Cornell looked down at his baggy blue jeans, and then he looked at his baggy blazer sleeves, hanging loosely from his limbs, as if made for a much larger man.

Whatever was happening to The Never Robbers was happening to him, too.

"Friends," Cornell said in a more congenial tone. "Maybe I will help you. But you might need to make a choice."

"What choice is that, chump?" Bishop Cafferty sneered.

"If you want in or out of the Madeline effect."

The three Never Robbers stared at their shoes and did not answer.

"If you stay out, this becomes the new reality, and you will continue to age until, well, I don't know what will happen," Cornell said.

The three Never Robbers looked at each other.

"If you go back, all the good you've done, and all the bad you've done will become undone," Cornell said. "You will return to the places you belong, and you will have no memory of each other, and you will lose the ability to alter memories."

"That's a difficult choice, Professor,"

Danny Tyler said.

"Can we think about it?" Mike Olsen asked.

"Can't you just fix it so we stop aging?" Bishop Cafferty said. "Everything used to be just fine."

Cornell shook his head. "That's not how the Madeline effect works. I think you're aging because people aren't remembering you. When memories of people fade.."

"...the people stop existing," Danny Tyler murmured.

Cornell held his pen over the notebook. "When did the aging begin?"

Mike Olson scratched his gray head. "Around the time we met you. I think."

Cornell wrote that down. "And when did you meet Molly Burton?"

"Today," Mike Olson said.

Danny Tyler held up an arthritic hand. "But it's been a really long day."

Cornell wrote that down, with effort, because it hurt to move his old stiff fingers. "But Molly wasn't aging. And she could remember you."

"That's right, Professor," Bishop

Cafferty said.

"And no one knows where she is now?"

He looked at all three Never Robbers. They looked at each other and then back at Cornell, shaking their heads and looking confused.

"Friends," Cornell said as patiently as a supernatural super sleuth can speak when he has an urgent supernatural mystery to solve. "You pulled me out of the Madeline effect so I could help you. But did you pull Molly out, too?"

"No," Danny Tyler said in a quiet voice.

"She just showed up," Mike Olsen said.

"She's robbed a lot of banks with us," Bishop Cafferty said. "Still, I don't even remember what she looks like."

Cornell wrote that down and then tapped his pen against the pad. "Maybe your aging isn't part of the Madeline effect. Maybe Molly is an evil spirit who's zapping your life force so she doesn't age. Maybe...

Just then a boy on a bicycle threw a newspaper at their feet and pedaled away. Cornell picked it up and read the headline out loud: "Prospect, Indiana's oldest citizen

Molly Burton died peacefully today at the age of 102."

"That blows your theory, Professor!" Bishop Cafferty sneered.

"Evil spirits don't die," Danny Tyler said.

"Now what happens to our life force?" Mike Olsen cried, looking panicky.

Cornell thought hard, and the gears in his head cranked very hard.

"This is a problem," Cornell said at long last. "Hop into my motor home. We are going to the cemetery."

CHAPTER FIVE: ON THE OTHER SIDE OF TIME

Cornell dropped the old box onto the kitchen floor and then lifted the next one onto the table and began sifting through its contents.

"I thought we were going to the cemetery, Professor," Bishop Cafferty sneered. "You've been digging through these boxes for hours."

"I didn't mean an actual cemetery," Cornell said.

He pointed to the boxes on the floor. Then he gestured at the empty cookie bags and old cookie crumbs strewn across the table. "I meant the place I keep my old research and unsolved cases."

He opened the flap of yet another tan envelope. "Eureka!" Cornell waved the envelope. "Here it is!"

"What is it?" Danny Tyler mumbled from the couch where he was dozing.

"My very first unsolved case: a little lost girl named Madeline Horton. She was last seen playing in the yard in Newport, Kansas." Cornell held up a yellowed, crumbling, stained newspaper clipping.

Mike Olsen raised his old head off the table where he had fallen asleep. "So the Madeline effect..."

"...was named for her!" Cornell exclaimed.

Cornell pulled out his notebook and began to write. "My friends, the police never solved this mystery because everyone forgot Madeline existed. But I kept this clipping as proof and vowed to solve the mystery one day."

He reached for a carrot stick and crunched as he thought, and the gears in his head cranked as he thought.

"Madeline and Molly have the same

last name," Cornell mused. "But what is the connection? What is...?"

He anxiously flipped back through his notes. "I don't remember. Why can't I remember? Who was my family? What was I doing before you stole my motor home?"

With effort, Bishop Cafferty gripped the table and pulled himself up. He pulled out an old pocket watch and looked very scared as he squeezed it.

"I can't hear it ticking," Bishop Cafferty mumbled. "I can't hear it ticking! I CAN'T HEAR IT..."

He was gone.

Danny Tyler sat up and pulled out his gold pocket watch. "Mike, what time do you have?"

Mike pulled out his old gold pocket watch. "A quarter past six."

Danny Tyler looked up. "I've got a quarter past five."

Cornell pulled out his pocket watch. It still read 6:15, the time he read in the jail.

But Cornell did notice something else, something as important as the time.

"Where did you get these pocket watches?" Cornell asked.

"We've had them with us since the diner," Danny Tyler said. "It was a gift from my wife."

"Hold them up," Cornell said.

All three gold watches looked almost the same. Danny's gleamed as if it was new. Mike's looked a little dull. Cornell's was tarnished with time.

Mike said, "I've had mine since I was young, so I'd always be mindful of the time. It has engravings on the front. See?"

Cornell took the watch and read: "To my son. May you be as great as its former owner."

Then Cornell held up his watch. "My grandfather gave it to me. On the front it said, " To my son. May you be as great as its former owner."

Mike frowned. "I know we've changed a lot of memories, but how to do you have my watch? And why does it look so old?"

"Your watch?" Cornell said. "This is not your watch. This was my Grandpa Mo's watch!"

Danny Tyler stroked his beard. "Mo? As in M.O.? As in, maybe, Mike Olsen?"

Mike Olsen's eyes grew very wide.

"Professor, I'm your grandfather?"

Cornell ignored the question. "Bishop Cafferty had a watch, too. Where did he get it."

"Don't know," Danny Tyler said, still looking at his own watch. "We never thought to ask."

CHAPTER SIX: IT'S MORE THAN A TIRE SWING

"I wonder," Cornell said, studying his watch. "I wonder if our aging dilemma is connected with these watches,"

He looked at the remaining two Never Robbers. "Did Molly Burton have this watch, too?"

"We don't know," Danny Tyler said.

Cornell put the watch back into his pocket and picked up his pen. "You never saw her with a watch?"

"No," Danny Tyler said.

Mike Olsen spoke up. "The only person who wasn't aging was Molly. Maybe we should go into town and ask about her. Or try to find her younger self. If we don't do something, one of us might disappear like Bishop Cafferty did!"

"Might as well," Cornell agreed. "We don't have any other clues."

Cornell and the last two Never Robbers very carefully hobbled down the steps and began to limp back toward the town square.

As they moved, the sky lightened, and Cornell felt the watch in his pocket buzz. He pulled it out and looked at it. Both watch hands rotated in unison around the watch face and stopped at twelve.

Cornell tilted the watch to the opposite side. The hands circled the face again and returned to twelve.

"My friends," Cornell said. "Are any of your watch hands moving?"

Danny Tyler and Mike Olsen pulled out their pocket watches.

"It's acting like a compass," Danny Tyler said.

"It wants us to go this way." Mike Olsen pointed right.

Wheezing with the effort, Cornell and

the two Never Robbers limped down the street, which gleamed with clean black tar in the morning sunlight.

They passed buildings with blue awnings and fresh white paint. Friendly shopkeepers smiled and waved to them as they opened their blinds.

A door banged open. A little boy with orange-red hair and orange-yellow freckles ran out carrying three well-polished wooden canes.

"Misters!" he cried. "Misters! Take these!"

Cornell thankfully accepted a cane from boys. And so did Danny Tyler and Mike Olsen.

"Thanks, Sonny," Mike Olsen said with a pat on the boy's head.

From the doorway of the Curtis Cane Shoppe, the boy's father waved and beamed.

Bracing themselves for support, Cornell and the remaining two Never Robbers staggered to the outskirts of town.

Every now and then, Cornell stopped, leaned on his cane, and checked his pocket watch.

When they came to a wide open field,

Danny Tyler croaked out, "I can't go any farther!"

Mike Olsen moaned in a gravelly voice, "Me, neither."

Danny Tyler's face was gaunt and transparent. He was bent like the letter "C."

Mike Olsen's had a little gray hair left. His skinny bowed legs shook from standing.

Cornell looked at his watch. "Friends, the watch has stopped ticking. We are here."

"Here?" Danny Tyler rasped. "There's nothing here but an old tire swing."

"Hanging from an even older tree," Mike Olsen gasped.

"Rest while I examine this tree," Cornell said.

Danny Tyler and Mike Olsen eased onto the grass, groaning with each inch.

Gripping his cane with weakening fingers, Cornell inched to the tree.

The tire had faded to gray, and its treads had worn smooth. It hung by a thick frayed rope off a thick tree with peeling bark.

Cornell leaned against the tree. Its

strong sturdiness belied its age.

He looked up. Even the branches pointing toward the clear blue sky looked pliable in their youthful appearance.

Each branch sprouted an abundance of smooth green leaves.

Cornell looked at the base of the trunk.

"Friends," he said. "I found something."

He removed a tiny magnifying glass from his left sock, mumbled, "Dittlia, romalny, careese," and peered through the giant magnifying glass to decipher the code at the bottom of the tree.

"Professor," Danny Tyler whispered. "I'm fading."

Cornell read the words aloud: "Come to me and rest."

"Professor!" Mike Olsen wailed. "Help Danny!"

With a burst of strength, Mike Olsen raised his cane and threw it. The cane tapped the swing, which began to wobble and then slowly turn.

Cornell whirled around. "Sir, never interrupt a supernatural super sleuth in his work. I'm on the verge of..."

"Look," Danny Tyler mumbled.

The tire swing picked up speed. Faster and faster it spun, sending a fierce wind across the three men.

Mike Olsen held up his watch. "Professor, look!"

The hands on Mike Olsen's watching were wildly gyrating.

"Mine's doing it, too!" Danny Tyler echoed in a faint voice.

Cornell pulled out his watch. The hands twisted in all directions.

"What's happening, Professor?" Mike Olsen cried.

The rope snapped; the tire fell onto the ground with a wobble and then lay flat.

A moment later, the tree fell with a crash.

Danny Tyler struggled to his feet. Mike Olsen struggled to his feet. And then they struggled to Cornell and the tire.

"That was dramatic," Danny Tyler said. "What caused it?"

As Cornell opened his mouth to reply, smoke wafted from the center of the tire. All three men crept close and peeped inside.

59

"It smells," Mike Olsen said, wrinkling his nose. "It smells like burnt rubber."

Cornell kicked the tire, and a blinding light shot out, and a great suction pulled him forward, an endless fall into a downward spiral.

As he fell, Cornell saw cracks of light, each followed by banks and robbers and getaways in speeding cars and horses and buggies.

A crack of ligh60t and Cornell saw Danny Tyler sitting inside Ford Theater in Washington D.C. with his wife, while one of the actors sneaked up behind him with a gun.

Light cracked, and Cornell saw Bishop Cafferty drop bags of gold dropped outside an orphanage.

Again light cracked, and Cornell opened his hand to receive an old gold pocket watch from Mike Olsen.

Another crack of light, and Cornell slumped in an easy chair, slurping an orange drink, and reading a newspaper story about a missing girl named Madelaine.

Crack, and a sobbing Mike Olsen ripped up a letter.

Crack, and a train sped Danny Tyler

away.

Crack, and Bishop Cafferty pounded on a farmhouse door.

Crack, and a screaming Molly Burton ran for a shovel.

More cracking light. More bank robberies, and with another crack of blinding light, Cornell landed with painful thud, his arms and legs tangled with those of Danny Tyler and Mike Olsen.

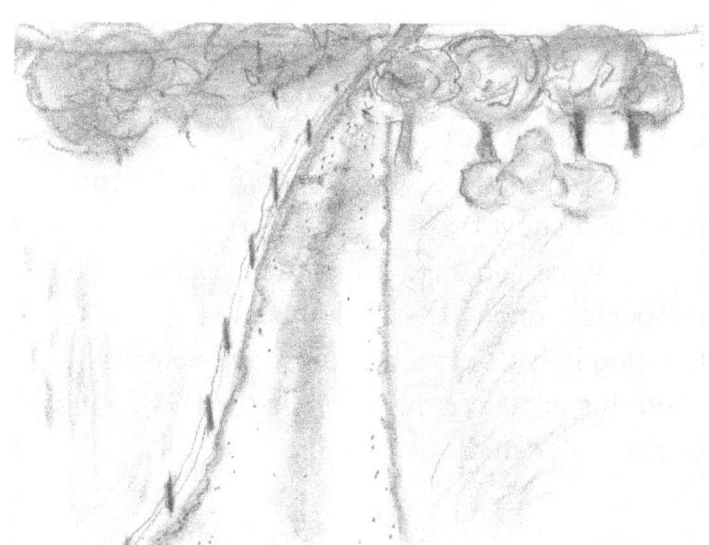

CHAPTER SEVEN: THAT OLE DIRT ROAD

"Ow!"
"Move your knee!"
"Get off my hand!"
With sharp kicks and elbow jabs, the three men extricated themselves and struggled to their feet, dusting off their clothes.
"Danny!" Mike!"
"Professor!" Danny Tyler and Mike Olsen exclaimed together.
Danny Tyler was very tall, very thin. He had a beard, a black suit, a stovetop hat, and he looked like Abraham Lincoln.

Mike Olsen, with his brown hair and freckles, was not too short and not too tall. He wasn't fat, and he wasn't thin. He was the type of person who could get lost in a crowd unless someone was specifically looking for him, which no one was.

Danny Tyler and Mike Olsen looked the way they looked when Cornell first met them, after they had robbed Prospect, Indiana's bank.

So Cornell assumed he, too, looked like himself: thick mop of curly hair, small, square black mustache, and just enough fat on his frame to fit his blue jeans. T-shirt, and colorful patchwork blazer.

Danny Tyler began to chuckle. "We dodged it again."

Mike Olsen grinned. "That we did."

Cornell looked around him on all sides. They were standing on a hard dirt road in a sunny green field.

The road had no signs. But Cornell no longer felt the need to hurry. He simply basked.

And studied the simple landscape.

And saw beyond the immediate in all directions.

He saw birds lay eggs. He saw the eggs hatch, fledglings fly; he saw them live and die.

He saw tiny shoots push out of the ground, grow sturdy and tall, and then fall to the axe to keep a family of four warm during a cold winter.

The air smelled of oncoming rain.

"Hello."

The voice came from the middle-age man suddenly standing with them. He wore dungarees, a brown plaid shirt, and kind eyes.

The man was with them, and yet he was detached from them.

He wasn't smiling, but he wasn't not smiling. His expression was mild and pleasant.

"Welcome to my road," the man said.

Cornell knew that voice. It was the voice from the tire swing, just not scary.

"I'm very happy you found my road because few do," the man continued. "But I'm not happy how you found it. That tire swing and tree have been around a very, very, very long time.

Danny Tyler and Mike Olsen glanced sheepishly at each other.

"We did not mean to break them," Danny Tyler said.

But Cornell was not intimidated.

"Sir, Cornell began, "I am the great..."

"Yes, yes, I know," the man interrupted. "You're the great Professor Cornell Dyer, world renowned super sleuth of supernatural mysteries."

Cornell stood taller and thrust out his chest. "So you've heard of me?"

"Yes, I know you well. Better, perhaps, than you know yourself."

Such a deep melodious voice, so unlike a voice Cornell had ever heard.

"Who are you?" Cornell asked, as he removed his notebook and clicked open his pen.

"I am He who is on the other side, the keeper of this road."

Cornell scowled. "That's not helpful."

"That is all the information you need."

Cornell tapped his pen impatiently. "Have you seen a young woman with curly reddish-blonde hair?"

"Yes."

Danny Tyler and Mike Olsen looked excitedly at each other.

"She has gone beyond," the man said.

Cornell sighed loudly. "Beyond where?"

The man waved his hand over the expanse. "Beyond this place, where you and others like you can no longer see her."

"What about a short man with black hair and a shorter temper?" Mike Olsen piped up. "His name is Bishop Cafferty. Have you seen him?"

"Yes, Mike Olsen. I know him very well. And I know you, too, very well."

Mike Olsen's jaw dropped.

"And I know all you have done and seen and heard and told. I know all the people you know, and I know your interactions with them. And I can tell you today you will be judged harder than the rest of them. Because you brought him."

The man pointed at Cornell.

"You brought the professor into the lifestyle you've all been living. And, yes, I know Bishop Cafferty, and you are correct: he does have a mean temper. His greed and anger have driven him from this place, and he has gone beyond. And he, too, will never be seen again by the likes of you."

Cornell snorted. The man obviously did not understand the persistence of supernatural super sleuths.

"Sir, show me the way to this 'beyond.'"

"That is not important now. Walk with me. You, too, Danny Tyler, although no one is upset with you."

Without looking back, the man headed down the road.

Danny Tyler shrugged his shoulders. "Why not?"

They set out after the man.

Soon, Cornell, the Never Robbers, and the man walked side by side on the narrow dirt road.

The man turned to Cornell, "I understand why you are here. You are here for good reasons. So I am inclined to help you. But first, let me check the time."

The man pulled out a pocket watch.

"Hey!" Cornell cried. "We all have..."

",,,the same watch. I know. Because it is the same watch."

Cornell scratched his face. "Four people with one watch? That's impossible!"

"As impossible as three men meeting up in different time periods?"

No one answered, not even Cornell. He was thinking, and the gears in his head cranked very hard.

"Cornell, great professor, I should shame you the most. For although you have seen the most, you believe the least."

"Who are you?" Cornell demanded.

"Who do you say I am?"

"I don't know! That's why I asked!"

"I am He who is on the other side. Names, and faces, and ideas, and traits, are all irrelevant. There is us and now, and this Ole Dirt Road. And we are all on a different journey than the one that led you here. You will not be going back that way. Neither will you come back here that way. "

Cornell wrote that down, which was difficult to do while he walked. "This is not our fault. The tree sucked us in. We're only trying to find two people who disappeared."

The man held up his hand. "You were by the tree because you cheated your way to the tree by using things that weren't yours."

"We did not!" Mike Olsen protested.

"The tree is mine. This road is mine. And I put them there long before any of you." The man sighed. "And they should have been there long after you. Hand me your watches."

"What!" Danny cried. "This was a gift from my wife."

"What!" Mike Olsen objected. "This was a gift from my father!"

Cornell shook his head. "Sir, whoever you are, you cannot have my watch. It was a gift from my grandfather."

But the man only said quietly. "You have misused them. Give them to me."

As if in a trance, Danny Tyler and Mike Olsen pulled out their watches and handed them to the man.

In a daze, Cornell felt his hand slink to his pocket, remove the watch, and hand it to the man.

But the only watch remaining in the man's hand was the man's watch. And he put that watch away.

"It's time," the man quietly said. "It's time to right your wrongs. You've changed too much, and the watches are erased."

"Fine!" Cornell exploded. "Keep the watches! I'll get out my own way!"

Cornell pulled an old brass compass from a blazer pocket and rudely shoved it near the man's face.

"This, sir, is my superlative super sleuth supernatural compass and tracking scope. It always points me exactly where I need to go."

With a happy little spin, the tiny golden needle pointed directly at the man.

Cornell shook the compass hard. But the needle refused to move. It stubbornly pointed to the man.

"Your device won't work your way here," the man said. "We are nearing our destination, and the sun shall soon set. I have many rooms and you may stay in them."

Mike Olsen chuckled. "You own a motel?"

"It's something like a motel."

"I don't want your hospitality!" Cornell shouted, fully frustrated. Supernatural sleuths do not like the hindering of their mission. "I am not afraid of this place, and I am not afraid of the dark."

He reached into his other back pocket and pulled out a giant flood light. "It's my own invention! It shines brighter than the sun powered with batteries made by Thomas Edison. It..."

"Your compasses and flashlights and sunstones and copper necklaces and magic orange juice for your olausopeller won't work here."

"What's a sunstone?" Mike Olsen asked.

Beyond them stood a flat, two-story, burnt orange building. In wide sea green script, a single word blinked on the roof: Motel.

Danny Tyler stroked his beard. "You own this?"

"My father does," the man said. "But I help."

The man led the way with Danny Tyler and Mike Olsen practically skipping after him.

Cornell held back, sulking. He tried the flashlight. But, as the man had predicted, it would not switch on.

So Cornell shoved it back into his pocket and reluctantly trudged inside.

Although the furniture was faded and frayed, the tile gleamed with fresh wax, and the air smelled of furniture polish

"Dinner and beverages will be sent to your room. The food is tasty, and the beds are comfortable. Rest well, for we will undo much tomorrow."

"But..."Mike Olsen said.

"Good night, gentlemen. If you need anything, just call. Someone is always listening.

CHAPTER EIGHT: A TRIP TO 1879

Cornell opened his eyes, yawned, stretched in the sunshine filtering past his curtains, and wondered when breakfast would arrive.

Probably soon. He gazed at the pile of his neatly folded clothes and decided to get dressed.

He was just tying the last shoe when he felt a lurch in his middle, the kind of lurch when speeding down a hill.

Everything went black.

Oh, no, Cornell thought.

The last time this happened, Cornell thought, I ended up in ancient Egypt, standing next to the pyramids.

Then he saw bright flashing lights.

Cornell was standing next to a gazebo with Danny Tyler and Mike Olsen.

Danny Tyler's shirt was unbuttoned.

Mike had shaving cream on his face and was holding a razor. His eyes widened.

"Guys," Mike whispered. "I know this place. It's my childhood home."

In the distance, thunder rumbled. A scream sounded. A maid ran past.

"He's gone!" the maid cried. "He's gone. The electricity burnt him to ash!"

The man stepped out from behind a bush. "Did everyone sleep well?"

Danny Tyler's shirt was now buttoned. Mike Olen's face was clean, and the razor was gone. Cornell was no longer hungry.

The man spread out his arms. "Welcome to 1879. Come walk with me."

Mike Olsen hesitated. "It's been a long time."

"Almost a hundred years," the man said. "Mike, in all your travels and in all your time, why did you not come back?"

Mike Olsen hung his head. "I don't know. I didn't care at the time. I wanted to see other places. I got distracted. I was having too much fun robbing banks that weren't there."

But the man only said quietly, "Your actions have affected many people."

To Cornell the man added, "This story has played out a thousand different ways over a thousand different years. You should not be here. But you are here because Mike brought you here."

The man gestured in the direction the maid had run. "It's time to go home."

"Home," Mike Olsen echoed. "Home."

Once again, the man led the way. This time, they walked in a single line, with Mike Olsen behind the man.

Cornell took a step and dawn broke. He took another and snow fell. He took another and the sidewalk cracked. A three-story house appeared in the dusk. He took a step, and a shingle fell. He took another, and a window cracked.

The house grew shabbier; the grass grew tall and full of weeds. Cornell felt the same. Danny Tyler looked the same.

But with each step into the future of his past, Mike Olsen aged a little more.

When they reached the back door, Mike Olsen had gray hair and a paunch at the middle.

Mike Olsen opened a creaking door into a dingy kitchen. The maid they heard screaming and saw running just minutes earlier now had white hair and wrinkles.

But she was humming a song and tidying up the kitchen.

"Mr. Olsen, shall I warm you a plate?"

Mike Olsen shook his head. "Did the letter arrive?"

She blinked back the tears. "Yes. The horrid bank people will be here tomorrow."

Cornell grabbed Mike Olsen's sleeve, but his hand passed through it. "Mike, what's happening?"

"How is she?" Mike Olsen asked.

"I've put her to bed."

"Professor," Danny Tyler whispered. "He can't see or hear us, can he?"

Mike Olsen walked out of the room. The man motioned for Cornell and Danny Tyler to follow Mike Olsen into the parlor.

When they arrived, Mike Olsen was sitting in a chair next to a bed, which was placed in the middle of the room.

A frail, elderly woman with wispy hair and brown spots on her face and scalp was propped up in that bed with the blankets pulled to her neck.

Mike Olsen patted her shriveled hand and did not speak. The woman, muttering, did not open her eyes.

'This is Mike's mother," the man said. "She has been very sad for a very long time."

"Why?" Cornell asked. "Mike Olsen, her son, is here."

"But Mike's father is not. When Mike disappeared and did not return, he died of a broken heart."

A baby's cry pierced the air.

The man looked at Cornell.

"On this night," the man said. "Your father was born. But he never knew this place, and neither did you. Every last cent was spent on her care."

They were back at the gazebo: the man, Cornell, and Danny Tyler."

Danny Tyler did not look old. But he did look translucent.

"Danny," the man said as Danny Tyler grew faint. "Your ideas, plans, and goals will

77

never come to pass. You will not see your sons become men. Your wife will not see some of your sons become men."

Danny Tyler faded into the air. Not even ash remained.

Everything turned hazy.

In the next instant, Cornell was standing behind his motor home.

On the same road where the Never Robbers had stolen it.

CHAPTER NINE: BEFORE THE THUNDER

The broken-down car at the side of the road was broken down no more. It zoomed past Cornell and his motor home without slowing down.

But Cornell caught a glimpse of its passengers: Bishop Cafferty and Molly Burton.

The man was sitting on his fender.

"Sir," Cornell said, utterly confused. "I thought we weren't interfering with time travel."

"We're not interfering with time travel," the man said. "We're repairing time.

The version you saw has ceased to exist."

"What happens to Bishop Cafferty? And Molly Burton, who needed my help?"

"They have gone beyond."

"I am a supernatural super sleuth. I deal with supernatural facts." Cornell sighed in loud exasperation and ran his hand through his hair. "Will you finally please give me a supernatural explanation?"

"They were stealing time. That was their crime. Not robbing banks that were never there. They were stealing other people's time and leaving only their ashes behind. Time has been repaired. They have gone beyond."

Cornell paid no attention to the vrooming traffic. He had to know the answer. He wanted to understand the mystery.

"So if time is fixed, does that mean Bishop Cafferty and Molly get to come back?"

"Perhaps," the man said. "Perhaps in another time. Hold out your hand."

Perplexed, Cornell did as the man instructed. The man set the pocket watch in it.

"This is yours," the man said. "It's just a watch, and it's yours to keep."

Cornell looked thoughtfully at the watch. And then he looked up at the man.

"What about Madeline?" Cornell asked.

"Ah, yes, Madeline, the little girl who started the Madeline effect. Madeline was the first to hear the thunder. I'm shocked you haven't connected the puzzle pieces. But you know what? Where there is punishment, there is also reward. And because you only became involved with the Never Robbers because you only wanted to help, I will reward you with the solution for your unsolved case."

Before Cornell could respond, the man said, "You and I, we are going to travel one more time."

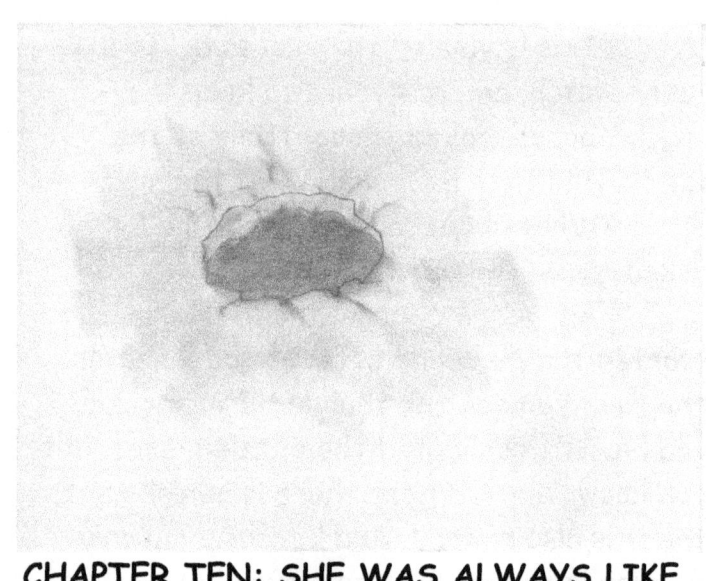

CHAPTER TEN: SHE WAS ALWAYS LIKE THAT

The sky shone brassy blue.
The grass had dried to brittle straw.
The ground was parched and cracked.
So was the wilted corn in the field.
The house was white with bare patches of wood.
But the house had a nice wide porch and a wide swing on the porch, and children's laughter bubbling through a propped-up open window.
The scene felt homey and pleasant, the type of scene where Cornell could park his motor home and stay for a long time.

Instinctively, Cornell headed for the porch. The man was already sitting on the swing.

From inside, a woman screeched, "I said, 'Be quiet!'"

The screen door sprang open, and two little girls, about eleven and seven, dashed out on their bare feet.

They wore faded calico dresses. And they both had curly reddish-blonde hair.

The girls flew down the stairs and sped around the side of the house. The woman ran out after them, swinging a broom.

"I'll teach you to make a ruckus and wake me up!"

The woman's eyes darted to the left and to the right. Her chest heaved with hard breaths. Finally stomped back into the house and began yelling again.

A weary man's voice answered.

Cornell heard giggling. Curious, he walked to the sound.

The older girl was placing a finger on the younger girl's lips.

"Come on, Maddie," she said. "Let's swing!"

"This is the day," the man said, now

83

next to Cornell, "that Madeline and Molly Burton's lives changed forever."

The shouting inside grew louder. Cornell peered in the window. The woman looked ferocious. The man looked disheveled and tired.

"He didn't always look like that," the man said. "But drought and poverty and a wife's illness can change a person."

Cornell turned away. "She doesn't look sick. Will she die?"

"It's not life-threatening. But she's always been this way."

The woman raced out the door with a big, long stick. This time, she did not pause to look this way and that way.

This time, she sprinted directly to the tire swing.

Cornell bolted after her.

He saw Molly pushing Maddie on the tire swing.

Molly was smiling.

Maddie was smiling.

"More, Molly," Maddie cried. "Push me more."

BOOM!
Flash!

The stick was gone.

Mom was there, holding a shovel and digging in the hard dirt.

Maddie was gone, too. Only a pile of ash remained.

Molly screamed and ran from the yard.

"Did you know the world is like Swiss cheese?" the man said.

Swiss cheese? Cornell wondered. What does the man mean by that?

The woman was gone. The shovel remained.

A black car drove up. Bishop Cafferty stepped out.

So did a hysterical Molly.

"Watch," the man said.

Puzzled, Cornell watched.

Bishop Cafferty strode up to the house and yanked on the locked door.

Screaming and crying, Molly ran to the tire swing.

"Eunice!" Bishop Cafferty shouted as he tugged on the knob and pounded on the jamb. "Open up! It's your brother!"

Molly grabbed the shovel and frantically started digging, tossing dirt everywhere.

"Molly!" she screamed. "Molly!"

"Danny Tyler and Mike Olsen also stumbled upon some of the holes in the world," the man said.

The scene changed again.

The house was gone, the farm was gone, and the tire swing and tree were also gone.

But Cornell remembered where Molly vanished. He decided to test the man's theory.

He walked back a few paces, turned around, and gave himself a running start before jumping right into the invisible hole.

His feet touched the ground. He was in the portal, but only up to his neck.

"What went wrong?" Cornell asked.

The man shrugged. "There are far less portals in the world today. And you don't always get to know the endings to other people's stories."

"But..."

"It's time to return to the motor home."

And just like that, Cornell was back in the driver's seat, key in hand.

As he slid the key into the ignition, ready for the next adventure, the pocket watch tumbled out of his pocket and onto the floor, and its back popped off.

As Cornell bent to retrieve the pieces, he noticed the watch contained a round black and white photograph of a woman with curly hair.

Wondering, Cornell removed the photo and read the inscription:

To my dearest Mike. Love, Madeline

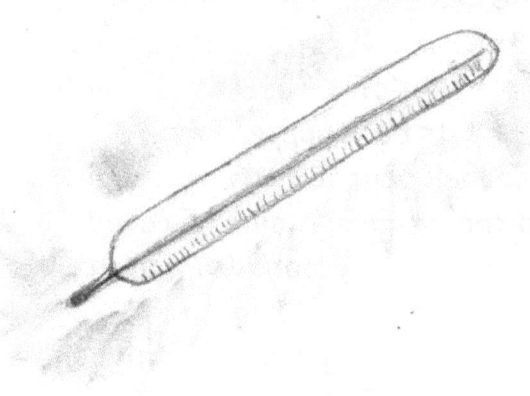

EPILOGUE

It was a busy morning, even for a Tuesday.

The receptionist had answered many phone calls, scheduled many appointments and written many receipts, so many her fingers hurt.

The nurse and the doctor had seen many patients, so many that the nurse's feet hurt from all her walking, and her starched white cap drooped over one ear.

The door banged open.

The receptionist jumped and smeared the ink. The nurse dropped a chart.

A man staggered across the room. He

had bushy black hair, a square mustache, and a bulky frame.

He was wearing blue jeans, a blue T-shirt, and colorful patchwork blazer.

"It's him!" the receptionist cried.

"I don't believe it," the nurse agreed. "After all this time."

"He has a lot of nerve!"

"Help me!" Cornell cried. "I'm very, very, very sick.

Calmly, the receptionist set aside her account book and picked up the chart.

Smiling, the nurse reached for the telephone and began to dial.

"Of course we'll help you," the receptionist said with a nod.

"McLouie's?" the nurse said. "I'd like one large pepperoni pizza."

The nurse covered the receiver and looked straight at Cornell. "Just as soon as we finish lunch."

THE FACTS IN THE FICTION

Many people had fears about electricity and electric light bulbs when they became prevalent in the 19th century.

Between 1878 and 1880, Thomas Edison and his team of researchers tested more than 3,000 bulbs before finding one he could patent.

The World Atlas at worldatlas.com has a list of famous bank robberies.

Time travel and traveling through portals is a common theme in science fiction stories, such as *The Time Machine* by H.G. Wells (1895).

Denise M. Baran-Unland is the author of the BryonySeries supernatural/literary trilogy for young and new adults, the Adventures of Cornell Dyer chapter book series for grade school children and the Bertrand the Mouse series for young children.
She has six adult children, three adult stepchildren, fourteen total grandchildren, six godchildren, and four cats.
She is the co-founder of WriteOn Joliet and previously taught features writing for a homeschool coop, with the students' work published in the co-op magazine and The Herald-News in Joliet.
Denise blogs daily and is currently the features editor at The Herald-News. To read her feature stories, visit www.theherald-news.com. For more information about Denise's fiction and to follow her on social media, visit www.bryonyseries.com.

Sue Midlock lives in Illinois with her husband and has been writing for 10 years. She started writing when the book "Twilight" first came out and fell in love with the paranormal genre.

Since then, she has written and finished her Rosewood Trilogy and just recently her anniversary edition, "Forever," which is the first book re-written for adults.

Her most recent releases are "Southern Shorts," which is an anthology of short stories about Dry Prong, Louisana and "Night Games."

Timothy Baran has enjoys cooking on professional and home levels. He also likes writing dark poetry and stories whose style mimics C. S. Lewis, his favorite author.
He is currently working on his first novel and a book of poetry.
But he especially loves his cat Midnight, whom he raised from a kitten.

www.ingramcontent.com/pod-product-compliance
Lightning Source LLC
Chambersburg PA
CBHW031412040426
42444CB00005B/529